Jackie Sheldon qualified and practised as a corporate solicitor in a large City firm before moving to the North-West where she worked at two commercial firms including Hammonds where she specialised in advising on corporate acquisitions.

Jackie has been teaching company law topics for over 20 years, is a Fellow of the Higher Education Academy, a Certified Management and Business Educator and has a Post Graduate Certificate in Professional Education. Jackie specialises in designing and delivering interactive, digestible and commercially relevant company law courses for solicitors, accountants and other professionals (including company directors and company secretaries).

Since 2022, Jackie has delivered over 50 live and interactive continuing professional development seminars on identity verification and the changes at Companies House for MBL Seminars. Jackie recognised that there was no practitioners text on the topic and wished to provide an analysis of the developing law, including how to practically navigate compliance.

A Practical Guide to Identity Verification Under the Economic Crime and Corporate Transparency Act 2023

A Practical Guide to Identity Verification Under the Economic Crime and Corporate Transparency Act 2023

Jackie Sheldon LLB (Hons), PGDip (Law), FHEA, PGCPE, CMBE
Solicitor, Director (*Maxlex Ventures Limited*)

Law Brief Publishing

Published 2026 by Law Brief Publishing, an imprint of Law Brief Publishing Ltd
30 The Parks
Minehead
Somerset
TA24 8BT

www.lawbriefpublishing.com

Paperback: 978-1-918241-23-5

PREFACE

Jackie qualified and practised as a corporate solicitor in a large City firm before moving to the North-West where she worked at two commercial firms including Hammonds where she specialised in advising on corporate acquisitions.

Jackie has been teaching for over 20 years, is a Fellow of the Higher Education Academy, a Certified Management and Business Educator and has a Post Graduate Certificate in Professional Education. To date, Jackie has delivered over 50 live and interactive continuing professional development ("CPD") seminars on identity verification and the changes at Companies House for MBL Seminars since 2022.

Jackie recognised that there was no practitioners text on the topic and wished to provide an analysis of the developing law, including how to practically navigate compliance.

Jackie would like to thank MBL Seminars for giving her the opportunity to develop the specialist training sessions that sit alongside this text.

Jackie would also like to thank her husband for all his support (and more than a quarter of a century of mugs of tea) and her martial arts sensei (Jake) for enabling Jackie to put into practice a significant number of the tips set out in this text.

Stated law is believed to be correct and up to date as at 27 February 2026.

Jackie Sheldon
February 2026

CONTENTS

CHAPTER ONE

WHY IDENTITY VERIFICATION IS BEING INTRODUCED (AND CONSEQUENCES FOR FAILURE TO COMPLY)

How the UK's framework for company registration and filing has been abused

The Companies House framework has historically been abused and used to conduct a variety of economic crimes; and it was in dire need of overhaul and control.

A company could be created and registered at Companies House in a few minutes, from anywhere, by anyone who had the ability to complete the relevant form and pay the small registration fee! Once a company has been registered at Companies House, an artificial person with its own legal personality has been born (and this artificial person can then conduct business, enter contracts, borrow money etc.).

Often fraudulent activity using companies and the register at Companies House has featured one or more of the following behaviours:

1. creation of a company deliberately to perpetrate fraud;

2. using an individual's personal details or addresses without consent; and/or

3. filing false information about a company to create a veneer of legitimacy.

Companies House has historically suffered problems with companies being formed for fraudulent purposes together with phoenix trading (which prevents creditors being able to claim on assets and customers unable to reclaim deposits and refunds).

Synthetic identities are also now becoming a more prevalent issue (and Chapter 7 explains this growing problem in more detail).

These historic problems stemmed from the requirement upon Companies House to accept all information filed in good faith (with no checks at all in place to confirm that the individual such as a director has consented to act, or if they were even a real person at all).

The system was also taken advantage of by using agents to form companies and to file on other peoples' behalf without conducting any form of robust due diligence or any anti-money laundering checks. It was supremely easy (and incredibly cheap and quick) to form a company, with the person filing based anywhere in the world, with no legitimate basis for the company creation.

A recent fraudulent example of misuse was where companies were established to fraudulently claim for government support during the Covid 19 pandemic. In 2021, HMRC seized twenty-six and a half million pounds in previously claimed furlough cash from a series of four fake companies which each claimed to have dozens of employees and had similar company names.

Ensuring all directors, people with significant control ("PSCs") and anyone presenting information to the register has an account with correct personal information, including a verified identity (and links showing all of their roles in one place) will make the legislation easier to enforce and officers traceable (as there will always be a verified natural person associated with an incorporation or filing).

Ensuring all roles are linked will have the dual benefit of enabling third parties (including consumers) to see what a director is doing and to recognise more easily when they may be dealing with fraudulent companies.

For example, if the register shows a director was linked to multiple companies with similar names that had all been wound up in quick succession, this can indicate fraudulent behaviour and allows the public to exercise caution in dealing with such companies. The corollary of this is that it can also positively help legitimate companies by showing third parties more detailed and reliable information and improving data on the public register which will go further to reassure third parties that they are genuine (as discussed in more detail below).

All the above has been reflected and supported by the enormous number of blogs, articles and announcements issued by Companies House. Andy King, Chief Executive and Registrar of Companies for England and Wales stated on 22 January 2026 that the "*introduction of identity verification will make it harder to use the register to create anonymous corporate structures that enable fraud, corruption or other criminal activity. Businesses use our data to carry out due diligence, access finance and add value to their products and services. So, making that data more accurate, up-to-date and reliable will support the government's broader mission for economic growth.*"[1]

Aims for identity verification

More than seven million individuals will be required to verify their identity. As noted above, historically, anyone, based anywhere in the world, could incorporate a company and file documents at Companies House, using fictitious names or false identities.

---

1 Andy King, 22 January 2026 – Becoming the trusted guardian of corporate transparency

Identity verification will address these historic crimes noted above by making it more difficult to register fictitious officers and enabling Companies House to know exactly who is filing documentation.

The Corporate Transparency and Register Reform White Paper Policy overview and response to final consultations was published in February 2022. It identified approximately half of all incorporations and filings are presented by third parties (such as solicitors, accountants and company formation agents (and that the majority are legitimate individuals and firms whose practice depends on their ability to incorporate companies and file documentation swiftly).[2]

However, it has also been recognised that offshore trust and company service providers are at high risk for being used for money laundering or terrorist financing schemes and the corresponding identity verification rules aim to ensure firms filing at Companies House comply with the new legislation (reducing these risks) whilst supporting legitimate activity.

Four objectives of ECCTA

The four objectives of the ECCTA aim to address the abusive behaviours discussed above:

Objective 1 – To ensure that any person who is required to deliver a document to the registrar does so (and that the requirements for proper delivery are complied with).

Objective 2 – To ensure that information contained in the register is accurate and that the register contains everything it ought to contain.

2 Corporate Transparency and Register Reform White Paper

Objective 3 – To ensure that records kept by the registrar do not create a false or misleading impression to members of the public.

Objective 4 – To prevent companies and others from carrying out unlawful activities, or facilitating the carrying out by others of unlawful activities [3]

Identity verification forms a key part in achieving these objectives. It underpins the goal of ensuring the integrity and reliability of the information available at Companies House. It is one of the elements introduced by the ECCTA, which will improve corporate transparency and tackle economic crime. This is also backed by "A blueprint for modern digital government: A long-term vision for digital public" published in January 2025 by Department of Science, Innovation and Technology which has six priorities to transform the government for a digital era (which includes expanding GOV.UK One Login).[4]

Improving the data on the public register

Companies House in October 2025 identified that the data on the public register is a valuable resource, aiding businesses making informed decisions and supporting transparency and that it plays a key role in the UK economy. Companies House data is estimated to be worth between one billion pounds and three billion pounds a year to users.[5]

Once individuals have verified their identity, this information is publicly available and can demonstrate legitimacy and credibility to third parties (including potentially enhancing the ability for companies to avail

3 Policy paper – Economic Crime and Corporate Transparency Act: outline transition plan for Companies House

4 A blueprint for modern digital government – January 2025

5 Why Identity Verification is Good for Business (October 2025) – Why identity verification is good for business – Companies House

themselves of financing and improving relationships with suppliers and creditors), together with assisting in identifying fraudulent behaviours as noted above.

For each company that an officer is appointed to, beneath the officers' details (which lists their name, role, date of birth, nationality, date of appointment and country of residence), there is now a new entry headed "Identity verification status". Once the officer has supplied their identity number and verification statement for that company, a green tick and entry in bold is added stating "**Verification requirements complete**".

By 3 October 2025, more than two million, seven hundred thousand people had signed a petition against biometric identity cards. Whether or not these digital identity cards proceed in the future, company officers should be reassured that identity verification does not create a digital identity – the purpose of identity verification is designed to prove that people on the register at Companies House (and those filing on behalf of others) are who they say they are.

Consequences for failure to comply

Companies House have indicated that the range of actions they will take for failure to comply follows four categories.

The first is that they will inform people of their obligations (so that individuals cannot plead they were not aware of the requirements), they will then nudge and guide people to enable compliance, deal with non-compliance and address fraud and criminal activity.

For communications, Companies House are using different methods to ensure all individuals impacted are aware of the requirements to verify their identity.

Firstly, they are utilising websites together with various social media channels. They have a bespoke website that focuses on all the changes to

UK company law (which is updated promptly to reflect any changes that occur). See Chapter 10: Useful Links at document C for this website. They also utilise a separate regular newsletter that provides useful and timely updates.

> Practical tip:
>
> If you are a practitioner and do not already subscribe to the Companies House newsletter, this text recommends subscribing.
>
> Link to subscribe can be found in Chapter 10: Useful Links at document A.
>
> You may also wish to consider following the Companies House official page on Linked In which can be a helpful source of discussion (and is also useful to see when the services may not be operating as expected).
>
> In addition, if you utilise social media, Companies House also has an official Facebook page that also shares regular short updates and reminders.

The above are general methods to staying informed. Companies House will also contact companies directly. Prior to a confirmation statement filing deadline, the relevant company will be emailed (using the registered email address for that company) to instruct them on the fact each of the directors must be verified by the filing deadline. Any advisor should check which email address is being used by each company and that the registered emails are being received (and read!). See below for a fictional email to a company with a confirmation statement becoming shortly due.

This has been reiterated frequently in official emails from Companies House. It is vital to ensure companies have chosen the most appropriate registered email address for the company and all registered email addresses have received an official email address with this information.

The official emails clearly indicate that the information is relevant to all companies registered in the UK and ask any third-party agents who receive the email on behalf of a company to forward it to all company directors of all companies they work with.

If there is any formal enforcement correspondence, a hard copy letter will be sent to the company's service address (which, to comply with the ECCTA, must be an "appropriate address" meaning that any letter sent to such address will come to the attention of a person acting on behalf of the company). In relation to PSC infractions, non-compliance letters will be posted to the residential address of the PSC concerned.

If individuals are struggling to achieve compliance, there is a lot of support available. The emails sent out to companies usually contain links to guidance on how to comply (See Chapter 3 for a fictional example of such an email), the guidance available online is free (and there are short, helpful videos) and Companies House also help via their contact centre.

When telephoning the Companies House contact centre directly, one of the options included within the initial menu is to select "one" if you are calling in relation to identity verification (to ensure the person calling is directed promptly to the team responsible).

If there is failure to comply with identity verification, the process will begin with a default letter to the individual concerned. This is a key point that is repeated throughout this text – it is the relevant officer's responsibility to comply and verify their own identity. The default letter will explain the offence and will also highlight that enforcement action may be taken without any further notice.

The enforcement action may include financial penalties, prosecution and referral to the Insolvency Service. Companies House will select what they deem the most appropriate, considering the nature of the non-compliance, circumstances set out in representations (see Chapter 3 below), and the seriousness of the transgression (including any previous patterns of non-compliance).

This enforcement action is directed at the individual who has failed to verify their identity (and potentially the company and its officers if they are directed by an unverified director under section 167(M) Companies Act 2006 – see Chapter 2 below). These consequences are separate to any consequences for failure to comply with the authorised corporate service provider ("ACSP") role, which is detailed in Chapter 6 below.

Fictional extract of an email for a company with a confirmation statement due within 4 weeks

This is an official email to the registered email address of XYZ LIMITED (1098765) from Companies House. If you're a third-party agent who has received this email on behalf of a company, please forward to the company director(s).

Your confirmation statement for XYZ LIMITED is due by X/XX/2026.

As a company director, you're legally responsible for filing this on time – even if your company is dormant or not trading, or if you use an agent or accountant to file on your behalf.

Verify your directors before you file

UK company law now requires all company directors to verify their identity.

If you've already verified your identity, you do not need to do it again – but you must provide your personal code for each role you hold.

Before you file your next confirmation statement you must make sure every company director has verified their identity and got their Companies House personal code and include the personal code for each director in your company's confirmation statement.

Your confirmation statement will be rejected if you do not complete these 2 steps.

If someone else files your confirmation statement, all directors must share their personal codes with them so they can include the details in your company's filing.

To verify your identity and get your personal code, go to: gov.uk/guidance/verify-your-identity-for-companies-house

You can verify online using GOV.UK One Login or through an Authorised Corporate Service Provider (ACSP), such as an accountant or solicitor.

If you've already verified and need guidance on where to find your code, go to: gov.uk/guidance/companies-house-personal-codes-for-identity-verification#where-to-find-your-personal-code

(Further instructions are also included within these emails, together with clear details surrounding the PSCs identity verification requirements and consequences for missing the deadline, which are reiterated as a financial penalty, the fact Companies House may remove the company from the register (which could impact the company business account and credit rating) and the public register will show the confirmation statement as overdue.

CHAPTER TWO

WHO IS REQUIRED TO VERIFY THEIR IDENTITY (INCLUDING HOW THE PROCESS FITS IN WITH APPOINTMENT OF NEW DIRECTORS AND WHO CAN FILE ON BEHALF OF WHOM)

Who will be required to verify their identity?

Companies House summaries the requirements by confirming anyone incorporating, running, owning or controlling a company in the UK must verify their identity.

The legislation, once fully in force, will apply to the following:

- New directors and PSCs of companies
- Existing directors and PSCs of companies
- Members of Limited Liability Partnerships ("LLPs")
- Presenters/people who file documentation at Companies House
- The senior person registering their firm to become an ACSP
- A registered officer (explained below) of each corporate general partner of limited partnerships under the Limited Partnership Act 1907

- A nominated director of corporate directors of companies
- A nominated director of corporate members of LLPs
- A nominated officer of corporate PSCs (technically known as Registrable Relevant Legal Entities("RRLEs")).

General partners of limited partnerships that are body corporates that have one or more corporate managing officers will be required to identify an individual to be the registered officer and named contact which must be notified to Companies House. It is this registered officer that must verify their identity.

There is currently no requirement for individual general partners of limited partnerships to have their identity verified.

Chapter 3 sets out the timing in relation to when each of these different people are required to verify.

Practical tip:

For transactional lawyers or lenders, where directors are to be appointed as part of a transaction, it is vital to ensure that the relevant individuals have verified their identity prior to completion of the relevant transaction and provided their personal codes to the advisors.

Consider making an update to the director's appointment letter (and relevant precedents) to confirm that this has been done and include a space for provision of their personal code and confirmation that they have not been disqualified.

It is also important to check that the warranties within the relevant sale and purchase agreement/loan agreement etc. include confirmation that the target company and its' officers have complied with the relevant provisions of the ECCTA.

Director's appointment process

Section 167M(1) Companies Act 2006 states an individual must not act as a director of a company unless their identity is verified (and under section 167M(3) Companies Act 2006, they commit an offence if they do so).

Section 167M(2) Companies Act 2006 states that a company must ensure that an individual does not act as a director unless the individual's identity is verified, and section 167M(4) Companies Act 2006, both the company and every officer of the company who is in default commits an offence. This also extends to shadow directors.

Although it is an offence (and may also give rise to a fine for those found liable), section 167M(6) Companies Act 2006 does clarify that the validity of the acts of the unverified director are not affected.

A company is also under an obligation under section 167(G) Companies Act 2006 to notify Companies House of the appointment of a new director on Form AP01, including the confirmation that they have been verified (pursuant to section 167G(3)(c) Companies Act 2006 and are not disqualified (section 167(G)(3)(d) Companies Act 2006).

The AP01 form contains the ability to confirm the individual's identity is verified and to provide their personal code.

Practical tip:

Combining the two requirements together – a director must not act unless they are verified and a company must notify Companies House of a new appointment within fourteen days beginning with the date of appointment (including the verification details).

The director therefore has fourteen days from the date of appointment (in accordance with company's articles of association) to be verified and the company must ensure they do not act as a director until they have verified their identity.

Who can file on behalf of whom?

The timings for this requirement are set out below in Chapter 3.

Section 1067A Companies Act 2006 sets out specific requirements as to who is permitted to file on behalf of whom.

> "(1) An individual may not deliver a document to the registrar on their own behalf unless:
>
> (a) their identity is verified, and
>
> (b) the document is accompanied by a statement to that effect.
>
> (2) An individual (A) may not deliver a document to the registrar on behalf of another person (B) who is of a description specified in column 1 of the following table unless:
>
> (a) the individual is of a description specified in the corresponding entry in column 2, and

(b) the document is accompanied by the statement specified in the corresponding entry in column 3.

1	*2*	*3*
Description of person on whose behalf document delivered (B)	*Description of individual who may deliver document on B's behalf (A)*	*Accompanying statement*
Firm	Individual who is an officer or employee of the firm and whose identity is verified (see section 1110A Companies Act 2006).	Statement by A— (a) that A is an officer or employee of the firm, (b) that A is delivering the document on the firm's behalf, and (c) that A's identity is verified.
Firm	Individual who is an officer or employee of a corporate officer of the firm and whose identity is verified.	Statement by A— (a) that A is an officer or employee of a corporate officer of the firm, (b) that A is delivering the document on the firm's behalf, and

		(c) that A's identity is verified.
Firm	Individual who is an authorised corporate service provider (see section 1098A Companies Act 2006).	Statement by A— (a) that A is an authorised corporate service provider, and (b) that A is delivering the document on the firm's behalf.
Firm	Individual who is an officer or employee of an authorised corporate service provider.	Statement by A— (a) that A is an officer or employee of an authorised corporate service provider, and (b) that A is delivering the document on the firm's behalf.
Individual	Individual whose identity is verified.	Statement by A— (a) that A is delivering the document on B's behalf, and (b) that A's identity is verified.

Individual	Individual who is an authorised corporate service provider.	Statement by A— (a) that A is an authorised corporate service provider, and (b) that A is delivering the document on B's behalf.
Individual	Individual who is an officer or employee of an authorised corporate service provider.	Statement by A— (a) that A is an officer or employee of an authorised corporate service provider, and (b) that A is delivering the document on B's behalf."

The table set out in the statute above may feel confusing to digest.

To summarise the requirements to date, a person may file on their own behalf if they are verified and are not disqualified (and are able to make the appropriate statement to that effect that their identity is verified).

If a filing is to be made on the behalf of another person (for example a firm or a company), it can be carried out by an officer or an employee (or officer or employee of a corporate officer) of the firm, whose identity is verified or an ACSP (or its officers or employees) (and they make a statement to that effect).

This extract from the legislation makes it clear that employees of an ACSP can file documents on behalf of another person without each separate employee requiring identity verification. This is also illustrated practically with the use of the authorised agent account discussed in Chapter 5.

It also flags another practical issue for group company secretaries. It illustrates based on the wording of the legislation that a group company secretary cannot file on behalf of another entity within the group unless they are also an officer or employee of that entity and their identity is verified.

Companies House are aware that this may cause difficulties for many groups; have stated that it is the subject of discussion and if any changes are to be made, the original intention was that it would be announced prior to Spring 2026. Considering the delay to the proposed Spring 2026 implementation (delays announced on 20 January 2026 and discussed in Chapter 3), this text assumes that this announcement and any intended changes may also be delayed.

Once this requirement is in force, the only work around the issue while we await a legislative resolution will be to either appoint someone with a verified identity as an officer or employee of each group entity (which may cause more logistical issues for the group) or to use an ACSP to make filings until the issue is resolved.

CHAPTER THREE

TIMING FOR VERIFICATION

The legislation is being implemented on a phased basis.

Voluntary verification

Since 18 March 2025, service providers who are registered for anti-money laundering purposes with a supervisor in the UK are able to register to become ACSPs, which allows them to provide identity verification services and confirm details to Companies House. There is now a list available at Companies House of all of the ACSPs registered to date.

From 8 April 2025, individuals were able to voluntarily verify their identity (See Chapter 4).

Compulsory verification for new incorporations

From 18 November 2025, all directors and PSCs for new incorporations will be required to verify their identity at the point of incorporation. You cannot complete the Form IN01 (and therefore cannot incorporate) without having completed the relevant verifications.

Part 2 of the Form IN01 now contains a statement that individual directors must have verified their identity in accordance with section 1110A of the Companies Act 2006. Box D5 (the individual directors' details) contains a requirement for the director to confirm the person appointed as a director has verified their identity in accordance with the

Companies Act 2006. The box beneath it requires the director's Companies House personal code (which is the 11-character code given to a person after they have verified their identity with Companies House).

Form IN01 also has an additional box (D6) that asks whether the name you have provided for the director matches their verified name (and if it does not match, they ask for additional information as to why, for example, legally changed name, preferred name, translation or naming convention (and they may contact the presenter for more information).

There are corresponding boxes from I6 in the Form IN01 for the individual PSCs verification statement and personal code.

<u>Practical tip:</u>

If you are incorporating companies for clients, ensure your onboarding documents and incorporation checklists require the directors and PSCs to confirm they have verified their identity, that the names supplied for the relevant officers/PSCs matches their identity documents and that they have each supplied you with their personal verification codes.

Transitional period for existing companies

The verifications requirements will be applied to all live companies with the transitional period allowing PSCs and directors to carry on their role and open a verified account.

The transition period of twelve months began on 18 November 2025 for existing companies, who will be required to provide IDV credentials for their directors and PSCs in accordance with differing timings.

Transitional period for existing directors

The transitional period for existing directors is linked to the company's confirmation statement (Form CS01). For example, if your company's confirmation statement is due on 31 June 2026, all directors must be verified by that date.

In a comparable way to the Form IN01, the personal code and verification statement will need to be provided for each director listed, within the confirmation statement. If the company cannot do this, the company will not be able to file their confirmation statement.

If someone else is filing the confirmation statement, all directors will need to share their personal codes with them in advance so they can be included in the company's filing. Most officers who have verified directly are likely to be aware of the need to share this code. When identity verification is successful, a pop-up message is provided advising the individual to only share their personal code with people filing on their behalf/people they trust).

> Practical tip:
>
> If you have a client who considers their personal code may have been shared without their consent or compromised in any other fashion, it is possible for Companies House to change their personal code.
>
> This new code will be sent to the individual concerned by email and their original/previous code will be cancelled.
>
> Companies House must be contacted directly to request this change.

If you are a director of multiple companies, you will need to provide the personal code and verification statement for each company separately using the same personal code each time, at the time of filing each relevant company's confirmation statement.

Individual PSCs

As noted above, for new incorporations, the PSC information is included within the Form IN01. The information below relates to existing companies.

Every PSC will have a fourteen-day period for each company they are a PSC of during which they must provide their personal code and verification statement. They cannot file earlier than the window allows. If they are a PSC of multiple companies, they will have separate windows for each company.

This period depends on whether they were registered as a PSC before 18 November 2025 and whether they are also a director of the company. The public register for each company shows the required filing window for each PSC so this should be checked and confirmed with the relevant PSCs.

> Practical tip:
>
> The compliance process for a PSC relies on the individual PSC taking action to notify Companies House of their personal code via a separate online service (it is not built-in to the company's annual filing obligations).
>
> If you are advising companies/clients/company secretarial teams that advise individual PSCs, ensure these individual PSCs are aware of these personal obligations as soon as possible.

Most firms would ideally have contacted their clients before these emails are circulated from Companies House, demonstrating a proactive approach to compliance.

See below for the sample fictional email that Companies House are circulating to the companies registered email addresses including the PSC warnings and deadlines.

Timing for a person with a dual role as both director and PSC

As noted above, for the directorship position, the personal code and identity verification statement must be provided in the Form CS01.

For the PSC position, the PSC must provide the personal code using the separate online service within fourteen days of the company's confirmation statement. This online service went live on 18 November 2025. It must be clear that this is two separate notification requirements. (Technically, although it is an online service, it is a Form VS01 that is being filed by or on behalf of the PSC). Again, if this person has multiple board and PSC roles, they will have multiple filing windows linked to each separate company's confirmation statement.

Timing for a person who is solely a PSC (and not a director)

The PSC must provide their personal code and verification statement within the first fourteen days of the PSC's birth month. For example, if their date of birth is 2 February, the fourteen-day period will run from 1 February to 14 February.

A common (and sensible!) query during CPD seminars has been why the deadline is linked to birth months (instead of confirmation statement deadlines). The thought process is that many PSCs may not be involved with the running of the company and linking the deadline to their birth month gives each person a clearly defined and identifiable period to comply.

> Practical tip:
>
> If for some reason the filing windows displayed at Companies House are not what was expected (for example the individual is also a director but it shows a filing window linked to their birthdate), this may be because Companies House was unable to match the director role with the PSC role. This often occurs due to name differences.
>
> In these circumstances, it is expected for the system to default to the timing window linked to the birth month despite the individual concerned having a dual role.
>
> Consider checking PSC and directorship details match completely to avoid any confusion and subsequent filing and identity verification delays in connecting personal codes to accounts.

Timing for a new PSC (i.e. became a PSC after 18 November 2025)

There is the option of providing the identity verification statement and personal code when the company notifies Companies House of the PSC within the PSC01 Form.

Contained within the PSC01 form, there is a new box A4 giving similar options to the Form IN01. If the PSC has already got a verified account (for example by virtual of another role with another company), they can simply provide their statement and personal code at this point within this form.

If they do not provide the personal code when they are added to the register, they must provide their personal code within fourteen days of being added to the Companies House register via the VS01 (the online service discussed above and see Chapter 10: Useful Links at Document O). Companies House will send the PSC a direction letter including the relevant deadline which will be sent out shortly after the PSC is added to the register.

Sample email (for a fictional company) from Companies House for PSCs

This is an official email to the company's registered email address from Companies House. If you're a third-party agent who has received this email on behalf of the company, please forward this message to the company directors.

[Tip: As noted above, checking these emails are being received is a useful practical compliance tool.]

ABC LTD's people with significant control need to verify their identity for Companies House

There's a new legal requirement for a company's people with significant control (PSCs) to verify their identity for Companies House, and to confirm that they have done so.

Instructions on how to do this can be found later in this email.

Who needs to do this, and when

All PSCs for ABC LTD need to do this.

There's a 14-day period during which each PSC must confirm their identity is verified. For PSCs that are also directors of this company, it's based on the company's confirmation statement date. For PSCs that are not directors of this company, it's the first 14 days of their birth month.

Based on the data we hold, these are the dates of each PSC's 14-day period:

- Mr Smith: 1 December 2025 – 11 January 2026[6]
- Mrs Bloggs: 1 February 2026 – 14 February 2026

For more information, read the guidance on when you need to verify your identity for Companies House (See Chapter 10: Useful Links at document H).

What happens if PSCs don't comply on time

They may face prosecution and a fine through the courts, or a financial penalty. In the future, we'll publish a note against their name, which will appear on this company's public record on the Companies House register.

How to meet identity verification requirements

There are 2 things each PSC needs to do to comply.

1. Verify their identity for Companies House, if they haven't already

[6] Mr Smith's due date is linked to ABC Limited's confirmation statement and shows a longer time frame for providing the identity verification code since two digital extensions were requested and granted. Mrs Bloggs due date is different as Mrs Bloggs is solely a PSC and was born in February, meaning Mrs Bloggs due date is linked to her birth month.

For information on how to do this, read the guidance on verifying your identity for Companies House. (See Chapter 10: Useful Links at document G).

After verifying, they'll be given a Companies House personal code. If they already have one, they do not need to verify again. The guidance on verifying your identity also includes instructions on where to find the personal code. (*Chapter 10: Useful Links at document J includes a link to a twenty-five second You Tube video created by Companies House instructing people on how to find this*).

2. Provide their Companies House personal code

This is so we can connect their verified identity to the PSC name on our records. We'll also ask them to tick a statement confirming they've verified their identity.

They can do this online using our "Provide identity verification details for a PSC service" (See Chapter 10: Useful Links at document O).

They need to do this even if they've already done it for other roles they have at this company, or at other companies.

If they cannot verify on time

They can request a 14-day extension using the "Provide identity verification details for a PSC" service (See Chapter 10: Useful Links at document P).

They must do this within their 14-day period.

Why do PSCs need to verify their identity?

This is a new legal requirement under the Economic Crime and Corporate Transparency Act 2023. All company directors and PSCs must verify their identity to prove they are who they say they are. This has been introduced to help prevent people using companies for illegal purposes.

You've received this email because you provided this registered email address to Companies House. You cannot unsubscribe from emails to the registered email address as this is a legal requirement under the Companies Act 2006. We will only use this email address to communicate about your company. The registered email address will not appear on the public register.

To change the company's registered email address, go to: https://find-and-update.company-information.service.gov.uk/registered-email-address

This is a no-reply email. If you need to contact us because you did not provide this email address as a registered email address, please email enquiries@companieshouse.gov.uk.

Timing for members of LLPs

The requirements for members of LLPs are in line with the requitements upon directors of companies.

Existing members of LLPs will have until the date of their confirmation statement to verify their identity (and will provide their personal code and verification statement as part of the confirmation statement). Members of LLPs appointed on or after 18 November 2025 will need to complete the identity verification process before their appointment can be registered at Companies House.

Proposed timing for Relevant Legal Entities

A relevant legal entity ("RLE") is a legal entity (such as another company) that would qualify as a PSC if they were a person (as they meet one or more of the PSC conditions). If they are a registerable RLE ("RRLE") (for example they are the first RLE on a chain of indirect ownership) they are subject to the same PSC regime requirements to provide their details to Companies House. Without requiring RRLE's to provide their conditions of control, there would be a significant gap in terms of transparency of the controlling mind of a company.

For RRLE's, instead of a fourteen-day window within which to provide identity verification information, they will have a period of twenty-eight days. As there is not one specific person (as an RRLE by its very nature is an entity), the RRLE will need to provide the name of a verified relevant officer. In relation to a company, this means a director of the RRLE. In relation to a legal entity the affairs of which are managed by its members, means one of those members and in relation to any other legal entity it means an officer of the entity whose functions correspond to that of a director.

The dates for this requirement have not yet been announced, but considering the delay announced in January 2026 to the Spring 2026 proposed deadlines, there is currently no indication of when this requirement will be introduced, but it would be advisable for any companies with RRLE's to prepare now for this implementation.

Practical tip:

For group structures, if there is one director who sits on most of the boards within the group, it may be sensible to consider providing their details for the "relevant officer".

If the relevant officer resigns, the details of a new relevant officer with a verified identity must be provided in their place.

If you advise companies who have RRLE's in their structure, consider advising them on who will be best placed to provide their details.

Timing for overseas companies with UK establishments

The identity verification rules apply to all individual directors registered at Companies House for the UK establishment, irrespective of whether they are involved in the UK business or not. Until the identity verification is completed, they may not act as a director of the company while in the UK. If they fail to get their identity verified and act as a director in the UK, both they and the company will commit an offence.

PSC rules do not apply to overseas companies with UK establishments, therefore there will be no identity verification requirements for PSCs for the establishments.

An individual who is a director of an overseas company with a UK establishment will have to have their identity verified before the UK establishment is registered at Companies House.

Existing directors of overseas companies with UK establishments will need to have their identity verified by the anniversary of the date of the opening of the UK establishment and must provide the identity verification details on the OS VS01 form.

Timing for presenters/third party agents

Identity verification will, in the future, become compulsory for anyone filing a document at Companies House (e.g. individuals) and any third-party agents filing on behalf of companies will need to be registered as ACSPs. This is designed to address many of the issues raised in Chapter 1.

Originally, it was proposed that these compulsory requirements would be in effect from Spring 2026. However, it was announced on 20 January 2026 that this anticipated Spring due date will be postponed. It will take place no earlier than November 2026 (and Companies House have confirmed they will give those impacted "*plenty of notice*" of when this change will happen.[7]

The reasoning for this delay is linked to allowing Companies House to complete the transition period of identity verification for existing directors and PSCs (and to also enable Companies House to address stakeholder feedback).

Extension of PSC IDV deadline digitally online (without evidence)

If an extension is required to a PSC verification deadline, there is the ability to request two separate fourteen-day extensions online. The application is straightforward and you merely need the company number and your reason for applying (for example, there is an error on the register at Companies House, and it will take the company time to submit the filings to correct this error).

As soon as the extension is applied for, a submission confirmation email will be sent confirming the date the submission was received, reference

7 Becoming the trusted guardian of corporate transparency – Andy King, 22 January 2026

number and filing type (e.g. extension request for PSC verification deadline). These should be retained should a further application be required. Companies House confirm the company will be emailed within two working days to confirm acceptance or rejection of the filing.

A follow up email will confirm if the request has been accepted and will clarify if it is the company's first or second extension, together with the new verification deadline. It will also explain which role the extension is for (e.g. only as a PSC of company X and does not apply to any other director or PSC roles held). A confirmation letter is also posted out to the PSC address on the records, and the public record is adjusted to show the new due date for the identity verification against the PSC.

Additional extensions for PSC deadline (after the initial two digital extensions)

For any further extensions, supporting evidence is required and the request and evidence must be submitted via an online form prior to the expiry of the current verification date. The PSC can apply themselves (or someone else can file this application on behalf of the PSC).

See Chapter 10: Useful Links at document P for the online form to request to extend the identity verification deadline for a PSC.

The request must be submitted before the current verification deadline has passed.

Information required before submitting a PSC extension request (after the initial two extensions)

To complete the form, you will require the PSC's full name (as it appears on the register at Companies House), the company number, a reason for the extension request (see below) and the supporting evidence.

Without supporting evidence, the request will be immediately rejected. A maximum of two documents may be provided (and these documents will depend on the reason for the extension request).

Examples of supporting evidence are set out below, based upon the reasons for the extension request. At least one document must be provided but there is the option to upload a second document. The application form is straightforward to complete.

Reasons a further extension may be requested

1.	Identity documents required have not yet arrived
2.	Individual is waiting to verify at a Post Office
3.	Medical treatment means the individual cannot verify on time
4.	Additional support or assistance is required
5.	Experiencing technical issues for a prolonged period of time
6.	PSC details are wrong on the register, and more time is required to file a correction

Documents required in support of a further extension

If identity documents required for the verification process have not arrived yet, a document will be required demonstrating that the application for these documents has been made, including a time and date of the application (for example an email confirmation of a passport application must include the time and date the email was received).

If the individual is waiting to verify their identity at the post office, the confirmation email discussed in Chapter 4 below in relation to Step 2 of the Post Office (assisted digital approach) (including the date the email was sent) may be deemed to be acceptable evidence.

If medical treatment means the individual's identity cannot be verified on time, a document confirming the medical treatment is required (including an official letterhead or verifiable stamp from a recognised medical professional for example a hospital letter or general practitioner. In addition, if additional support or assistance is required to verify the identity (and this support has been arranged), a document confirming the reasons for additional support is required (for example a report from an educational professional, educational psychologist, medical professional, occupational therapist or online screening product).

If the reason behind the extension request is experiencing technical issues (for a prolonged period), evidence will be needed in the form of an email or screenshot from a service provider outlining the details of the technical fault and the date and time that it occurred.

Finally, if the reason that the extension is requested is due to the PSC details on the company record being incorrect and more time is needed to file a correction, a document or screengrab that shows a correction filing has been submitted (which could include a copy of the forms or something that illustrates the reference number for the filing).

Practical tips:

Companies House are not providing any exceptions or leniency if there are historic inaccuracies with the information at Companies House.

For example, if the day of a date of birth was incorrectly provided to Companies House on incorporation, the personal identity verification code will not link/connect to the person as the details do not match. The information held at Companies House will need to be corrected before the identity verification code is accepted.

If you are filing an RP01 or RP04 (which currently must be filed in hard copy and will not be accepted in electronic form without express approval from a member of the second filings team), ensure a copy of the form is made and obtain proof of postage at the Post Office. Without this, there will be no evidence that a correction has been posted.

If you are correcting information relating to names and dates of births etc., Companies House filing team do require evidence such as a passport to support the correction (but have confirmed copies are acceptable for this).

If you are close to an identity verification deadline, it is possible to contact Companies House to explain the urgency and discuss how this can be sped up. However, this text would always recommend seeking an extension in any event, as there is no guarantee an amended filing is accepted and corrections can take time to process.

What happens after a further request for an extension to a verification deadline has been submitted

Companies House will review the evidence and will email the company at the registered email address to confirm whether the request has been accepted or rejected. The decision is at the discretion of the registrar (and there is currently no information as to how this may be appealed).

See Chapter 6 on Companies House approach to non-compliance if it is not accepted. If the request is accepted, an additional fourteen days will be granted to provide the identity verification details, beginning from the end of the current fourteen-day period.

CHAPTER FOUR

HOW TO VERIFY DIRECTLY WITH COMPANIES HOUSE

Three ways of verifying directly with Companies House

The service provided is via GOV.UK One Login and it is free of charge.

The service asks the user some brief questions to analyse the best way for each user to verify their identity. This relies on the user answering questions about themselves and not their company.

The three options available are:

1. Using the GOV.UK One app
2. Answering security questions online
3. Creating a GOV.UK One Login and entering details from the photographic identification before attending a participating Post Office.

If an individual is unable to use any of the three options, the only alternative method is to engage an ACSP to verify their identity on their behalf (e.g. an accountant or solicitor who is registered as an ACSP) (which will come with a fee for their services).

It should be noted that a person can use the first or second option above from any country, but the ACSP must be a registered ACSP with Companies House (see Chapter 5 below) which includes the ACSP always being registered with at least one UK anti-money laundering supervisory body.

An individual can ask their existing advisors if they are registered as an ACSP and there is also a list of ACSPs available at Companies House.

See Chapter 7 below for the documents each person needs to provide to an ACSP and how an ACSP can verify a client's identity.

An impact assessment published in 2024 identified that it could be more difficult to verify the identities of some directors and PSCs. These individuals were identified as "harder to verify", for example, overseas residents with non-biometric passports or those with unknown nationalities and residencies. The impact assessment classed officers as "easy to verify" or "harder to verify" and estimated that 94.5% of officers will fall within the "easy to verify" category, leaving 5.5% as "harder to verify". In addition, later analysis by Companies House has estimated the "harder to verify" category as potentially as low as 2.4% of officers. The verification method for this small proportion of officers will need to be via an ACSP (but this will be reviewed on an ongoing basis, and alternatives may be developed over time)[8]

GOV.UK One App (Standard digital approach)

An individual can verify themselves online with GOV.UK One Login if they have one of a specific set of photographic identification as follows:

1. Biometric passport from any country (a biometric passport has a small rectangular symbol on the front cover. All UK passports issued after 2006 are biometric, but this means that a person

[8] The Registrar (Identity Verification and Authorised Corporate Service Providers) Regulations 2024 Impact Assessment 28 February 2024

anywhere in the world with a biometric passport can verify their identity with Companies House)

2. UK photo driving licence (which may be a full or provisional licence)

3. UK biometric residence permit or UK biometric residence card

4. UK Frontier Worker permit

Before starting the process, the individual will also need to be able to supply their current address together with the year they moved into that address and to sign in to or create a GOV.UK One Login.

Creating a GOV.UK One Login account is straightforward. The individual simply navigates to the GOV.UK One Loging site to set up an account using a personal email address (see below for practical suggestions and tips in relation to email addresses utilised).

If the individual already has an existing Companies House account (for example, for historic WebFiling), if the individual has not already connected this account to their GOV.UK One Login, it will prompt the connection of these two accounts by entering the Companies House password (and this connection will only work if the same email address is used for both Companies House and GOV.UK One Login). This will only need to be done once and will save all the existing Companies House account information to the GOV.UK One account (see below for a step-by-step guide plus other tips for WebFiling accounts).

Practical tips:

Historic GOV.UK One Login accounts

Many clients were unaware that they had historically created a GOV.UK One Login, as this account can and may be used to access one hundred and ten other government services (such as applying for a disclosure and barring service check). Clients should check and confirm the email address they used to access this service.

If other people shared or used the same address to also access GOV.UK One Login, they should now create their own account using a different email address as an email address can only be used once to verify a person's identity.

Technical work around suggestion

Many delegates have reported struggling with the app. This tip may help! Begin the entire identity verification process on a laptop or desktop. (You will use your device after beginning the process to scan a QR code, scan your identity document and take a picture of yourself).

Do NOT download the app to your device first. If you have already got the app, consider deleting it and restarting the process below.

Go to the GOV.UK One Login page, set up the account (if you do not have one already) and then scan the QR code that appears on the screen with your device (which will then download the app to your device). This ensures your device connects seamlessly with the account open on your laptop.

How to access your WebFiling or Companies House account

It is important that the email address historically used to sign into WebFiling is current (and accessible). This can be updated by selecting "change account details" after signing into the WebFiling account. The link to access WebFiling can be found in Chapter 10 at document R.

If a separate Companies House account is used for the "Find and Update" company information service, this MUST be the same email address for both accounts. If they are not the same, one must be changed as they need to match. Companies House has a clear warning that states "***You will lose any existing information if you do not use the same email address to sign in to each account. You must also use the same email address for your GOV.UK One Login.***"

As soon as the person accessing the services signs in to the WebFiling account, there is a redirection to connect the account with GOV.UK One Login.

If they already have a GOV.UK One Login, they will be able to sign in and connect their account.

If they do not have one, they will be prompted at this point to create one. If they have a separate Companies House account for the "Find and Update" company information service, both accounts can be connected to the GOV.UK One Login at the same time.

Only one person can connect each WebFiling account to their GOV.UK One Login (which may be a practical issue if WebFiling accounts were shared). See below for how to connect the accounts.

Check if there is anyone who shares access to these accounts (and they will need to create a separate GOV.UK One Login with a different email address. It is Important to be aware that they will not be able to use the previously shared accounts to access the company information.

How to connect existing accounts

Begin by logging in to the WebFiing page. To connect the accounts:

1. Create or sign in to your GOV.UK One Login on the screen that appears after logging in to WebFiling.

2. Companies House will then ask you to enter a security code that they will send to the email address discussed above.

How to change email addresses

As noted above, if accounts use different email addresses, they need to be updated to be the same prior to connection. Instructions for how to update the WebFiling email address are above.

- For Companies House account emails changes: update your Companies House account email address

- For GOV.UK One Login email address changes: update your GOV.UK One Login email address

Answering security questions online (Standard digital approach)

Many advisors have clients who may, for several reasons, not possess photo identification.

Without the specific photo identification listed above, the individual will not be able to use the GOV.UK One app. However, it is still potentially viable to prove identity via GOV.UK One Login and use the standard digital approach by answering security questions instead. This can be used if the individual has either photo identification **or** a current account with a UK bank or building society.

Practical tips:

The security questions must be answered correctly for this method to be successful. Any mistake in the answers means the individual cannot use this method again.

If the individual considers the questions have been answered correctly but the identity verification was not successful, the individual may wish to obtain a copy of their credit file/report to check for any errors (as GOV.UK One Login checks the answers provided by the individual against information held by Experian which is compiled from information in the individuals credit file). (Experian is highlighted in the privacy notice below).

Any credit reference agency can be contacted to obtain a copy of the credit file, and it is free of charge. It does not have to be Experian (although this text would suggest it would make sense to use Experian directly as this is the source utilised by GOV.UK One Login). See Chapter 10: Useful Links at document K for how to obtain Experian credit report for free.

The credit file should be checked carefully for any errors such as incorrect addresses, misspelt names or old accounts.

If this route is being utilised, one issue is whether the individual has different names on different identity documents.

Identity can be provided using an identity document with any of the individual's names on it. However, the name on the document must match the details that Experian keeps about that individual, including any middle names or initials, making the practical tip above of a credit search even more valid. If the names do not precisely match, the individual will not be able to prove their identity with this route.

An extract from the privacy notice (attached in full below) highlights this as it states "*if you prove your identity without photo ID, we may ask you to provide your name and the account number and sort code of a UK current bank account in your name. We then check your UK current account details against the details held by banks across the UK, using a checking service provided by Experian.*

When Experian have completed the check, they tell us:

- *whether the information you provided matches or not*
- *where the name you provided is a partial match to banking records, the official name on record.*"

Attending a Post Office (Assisted digital approach)

The Post Office option is only available for individuals who have a home address in the UK. There is a specific order that must be followed to use this free service which is set out below.

Step 1. Enter the photo identity details in the applicable "Verify your identity for Companies House" service and select a participating Post Office. (Please note the individual does not have to attend the selected Post Office for Step 3).

Step 2: Obtain your Post Office customer letter

Once you have completed Step 1, the individual will receive a confirmation email. Included within the email is a link to download the customer letter to their device. It is possible to opt for a hard copy sent by post (but this can take up to six working days to arrive and is therefore a risk that the letter may arrive after the date set out in the letter and discussed below). This letter contains a QR code that will be utilised in Step 4.

Step 3: Attend any participating Post Office with confirmation letter and original photo identity.

The individual must attend a Post Office that offers in branch verification with their customer letter (either electronically on their device or printed). The person must take the original photo identity (digital images will not be accepted, neither will photocopies). The individual must attend by the date included in the customer letter (which is usually around fifteen days from when the confirmation email is sent out)

Step 4: Get the QR code scanned

A member of staff from the Post Office will scan the QR code included in the customer letter which confirms they are verifying their identity for Companies House. As noted above, there is no charge for this service.

Step 5: Photo taken/ID scanned

A member of staff from the Post Office will then take the individuals photo and scan their photo identification.

Step 6: Check emails for the result

An email will be sent from GOV.UK One Login with the result of the identity check (expected usually within 1 day of attending the Post Office). This email includes a link to sign in to the GOV.UK One Login. Once signed in, the individual then returns to the Companies House service to see the verification result.

If the check has been successful, the message will state "You have already proved your identity" and the individual then selects "continue" which will then reveal the Companies House personal code. The individual can also locate their code later in the "manage account" section of the Companies House account.

If the check was not successful, the email will contain guidance on how to proceed.

Privacy concerns/How GOV.UK One use the data provided

Many firms have raised privacy concerns as something deeply important to clients and it is therefore useful to be aware of what happens to data when personal data is provided as part of the verification process.

GOV.UK One Login is provided by the Government Digital Service which is part of the Department for Science, Innovation and Technology ("DSIT"). DSIT is the data controller for the personal data individuals provide when using the GOV.UK One login.

The full privacy notice can be found here: GOV.UK One Login: privacy notice – GOV.UK. It details who the specialist identity checking service providers are, the checks that are made, the documents and information that may be collected (and for how long) and who the data is shared with.

CHAPTER FIVE

HOW TO BECOME AN AUTHORISED CORPORATE SERVICE PROVIDER

There are several steps involved in becoming an ACSP. Another term used for ACSPs by Companies House is authorised agents. The registration process went live on 18 March 2025.

Step 1 – Before registration

Prior to registration, the agent must already be registered with at least one anti-money laundering supervisory body that regulates the agent's industry sector (for example the Solicitors Regulation Authority for solicitors). There are some businesses that are not eligible for anti-money laundering supervision.

During the transitional period, agents only need to register as ACSP's if they wish to verify the identity of their clients for Companies House. As noted above, in the future, all agents who wish to file documents for the clients at Companies House will need to register as ACSPs (but this will not be before November 2026).

There are currently twenty-five anti-money laundering supervisory bodies in the UK – the full list can be found in Chapter 10: Useful Links at document E.

Practical tip:

One of the most common reasons for rejection of applications to become ACSP's is due to the information held with the supervisory body failing to match the information held at Companies House about the agent.

Before beginning the application, check the name that the anti-money laundering supervisor body holds for your entity. If it does not match the company name that is shown at Companies House (for example it is in a different name), update this with your supervisory body in advance. Do not start the application before this has been corrected.

If the agent is unsure where to find the anti-money laundering details, depending on the supervisory body, it may be located on the individuals practising certificate, correspondence from the supervisory body, or their online register.

Be aware that the anti-money laundering supervisory body may have a different name for these details such as a firm identity or number, regulation identity or AML identity.

If the individual is still unsure, it is vital to contact the anti-money laundering supervisory body to confirm this before commencing the application. Contact details for every supervisory body are included in the list of supervisory bodies (See Chapter 10: Useful Links at document E).

Based on anecdotal reports from various firms of different types applying to register as an ACSP, the firm may wish to contact their relevant supervisory body in advance in any event, to ensure they are aware of the application and to avoid any delay in the supervisory body providing the relevant details to Companies House.

Step 2 – How to register as an ACSP

To register as an ACSP, the Companies House link to apply must be used (See Chapter 10: Useful Links at document I).

Both sole traders and businesses can register as ACSPs. Whatever the form of business, a person with a senior role must apply (for example, a director of a company, a general partner of a limited partnership or a member of a limited liability partnership).

This person must have verified their identity before beginning the application process (and will therefore need to create a GOV.UK One Login as detailed in Chapter 4).

The person making the application is free to add any other employees to their account once registration is complete (see Step 3 below). These employees will not need to verify their identity but will need to create their own account. They will be able to carry out all the services on behalf the ACSP such as filing forms and accounts for clients and identity verification for clients if this is being done (see Chapter 6 for the considerations in terms of risk for firms verifying for clients).

After signing in to GOV.UK One Login, the person will then provide details which will depend on the type of entity they are registering as an ACSP.

If the person is applying to register either a limited company or a limited liability partnership, they will need to provide the company number, the company authentication code (see below for explanation of this code), correspondence address and an email address for correspondence. It is also optional to provide the business sector operated in. If the person is a sole trader (for example self-employed and registered with HMRC for self-assessment), the information to be provided is slightly different. Sole traders must provide their name, any business name used, their date of birth, nationality, country the live in (including which part of the UK), correspondence address, email address for correspondence and if the supervisory body holds their name, their business name or both names. Again, as with companies and limited liability partnerships, it is optional to provide the business sector operated in.

There are also other forms of business that may wish to register for example, limited partnerships, partnerships, other corporate bodies (other than limited companies and limited liability partnerships) and unincorporated entities (not including sole traders). These entities will need to provide a business name, UK business address, correspondence address and an email address for correspondence. Again, the business sector operated in is optional. If the anti-money laundering registration is with the individual name, this must be provided (otherwise Companies House will check the anti-money laundering supervisory body holds the correct business name).

Company authentication code

Remember that the company authentication code is different to the personal code received when verifying identities.

This is a six-digit alphanumeric code historically issued by Companies House to each company which is used to authorise filing information online. If the company has previously filed documents online, it will already have this code (as it is the equivalent of a director's signature).

If the company does not have a code, one can be requested following the link set out in Chapter 10: Useful Links at document B (but please note that this is sent out by post and can take up to ten days to arrive).

Once all the information is provided, the individual making the application will need to confirm that they accept the legal responsibilities as authorised agent and pay the appropriate fee for registration.

See Chapter 6 for more information in relation to this (and the consequences for failure to comply with their legal responsibilities).

Up to 1 February 2026, the fee was £55. After the fee increase on 1 February 2026, the new fee is £63.

Top tips for a successful application (using Institute of Chartered Accountants in England and Wales ("ICAEW") as the anti-money laundering supervisory example

This example utilises the steps outlined above.

Step 1 – Before registration

To ensure the application is successful it is vital that the Companies House information about the firm matches with the ICAEW information. Some recommended checks are set out below to avoid common mistakes that may cause a delay or rejection to an application.

Check that the firm applying is supervised by a UK anti-money laundering supervisory body. ICAEW is included within the list of supervisory bodies (See Chapter 10: Useful Links at document E) and the contact details of the relevant team are also provided within this list.

Merely being an ICAEW member or having ICAEW as the firm's regulator does not automatically make ICAEW as the firm's anti-money laundering supervisor so it is vital to check this in advance before beginning the application.

As noted above, details about the firm will be required including name (this must be the legal name and NOT a trading name, trading names are not shared with Companies House), address and email address as well as the company number, name of the anti-money laundering supervisory body and anti-money laundering membership number or identification. (See below for more information about the correct number).

Check the firm's annual return for the accurate information and ensure this is replicated precisely.

A common issue to date is firms providing the incorrect anti-money laundering supervisory number, so it is important to ensure the correct number is located before beginning.

It must be the firm's number and not the officer making the application's personal number. This can be found on the firm's annual return and will begin with C0 (zero) or less commonly for some older firms it may begin with A0 (zero). It does not begin with L0 which is usually the reference numbers given by ICAEW.

Step 2 – How to register – top tips

Within the application, the person applying must answer the question to "What type of business are you registering?"

The options are limited company, limited partnership, limited liability partnership, partnership not registered with Companies House, sole trader or other. If you select "other", the options that appear are either corporate body registered with Companies House or unincorporated entity.

One common pitfall is selecting "sole trader" rather than "unincorporated entity" for sole practitioners. Again, this may cause a delay or rejection in the application.

Step 3 – After registration as an ACSP

Once the application has been accepted by Companies House, the business that applied will be registered as an authorised agent.

Companies House will create a separate authorised digital agent account for this business and will provide a unique identity number for the ACSP. See Chapter 6 for how this account can be used.

Interestingly, Companies House guidance originally stated they will not publish information to show that a business has registered as an ACSP.

However, there is a list of businesses that have registered as ACSPs (and who have requested that their information be included within this list) (See Chapter 10: Useful Links at document M). This therefore means that the list is not exhaustive, and a firm may have registered as an ACSP but did not wish to be included within this list.

Companies House do not recommend or endorse any ACSP included within the non-exhaustive list, so there may be little to gain from being included within the list, other than to show individuals who are searching for an ACSP that the firm has been successfully registered.

It should also be noted although there is no definitive list of those registered, that there is, however, a publicly available list of any ACSP that has been suspended or ceased to be authorised (see Chapter 6 for more information).

As at December 2025, fifty ACSPs had already been suspended and twenty-seven ACSPs have already acquired "ceased" status. The list is updated with any changes every two weeks (so it is important to be aware that even if an ACSP has been suspended or ceased, it can take up to two weeks for them to be added to the list.

There is no information available at Companies House to explain the reasons behind these actions. A firm may be ceased if they do not comply with legal requirements or if they inform Companies House that they do not want to be registered.

If a particular firm or person has been ceased or suspended, the only way of delving into the action further is to research the firm independently (for example, in selecting a random ceased ACSP on the public list, further research illustrated that despite their website still proudly declaring the firm was a registered ACSP, the firm had in fact ceased to trade). For many suspended and/or ceased ACSPs, it is not always possible to discover the reasons behind the suspension or cessation.

There will also be information available at Companies House where a person uses as ACSP to verify their identity (as it will show the name of the agent that verified them together with the names of the relevant anti-money laundering supervisory bodies the ACSP is supervised by).

See Chapter 6 for considerations in relation to risk and internal policy.

CHAPTER SIX

HOW TO COMPLY WITH YOUR REQUIREMENTS AS AN AUTHORISED CORPORATE SERVICE PROVIDER (AND CONSEQUENCES OF FAILURE TO COMPLY)

ACSPs legal responsibilities

As part of the registration process, the firm/sole trader will have to confirm it accepts its legal responsibilities as an ACSP.

It is therefore vitally important that those who may be liable for breach are aware of what these responsibilities are and measures are put in place to ensure continued compliance.

There are four key obligations upon ACSPs (that span a wider range of requirements).

Firstly, an ACSP must always be registered with at least one UK anti-money laundering supervisory body.

Secondly, the ACSP must tell Companies House about any changes to the ACSP's details within fourteen days. This obligation can be managed via the ACSP's authorised agent account (see below for more details in relation to operating this account). It includes any changes to their information held at Companies House, including if the ACSP is no longer registered with a UK anti-money laundering supervisory body. Failure to comply within the time limit is an offence. To update the

ACSP's details, an account owner (see below for more information) can use the authorised agent account to "View and update the authorised agent's details".

Thirdly, the ACSP must keep records and provide more information about Companies House filings, identity checks (if the ACSP verifies an individual's identity for Companies House) or to prove the ACSP is complying with their legal responsibilities.

The fourth and final obligation is that if the ACSP verifies identities for Companies House, they must keep records of any identity checks for seven years (see Chapter 7 for more information).

Collection of guidance for ACSPs

A common complaint from current users is that finding the necessary log ins and links can be time consuming. Companies House have reacted to feedback and have produced an area solely for guidance for ACSPs, including a link to access their authorised agent account. See Chapter 10: Useful Links at document D.

How to use the ACSP authorised agent account

When the firm's officers sign into their own Companies House accounts (as noted above, to verify their own identity, each person must create their own GOV.UK One Log in), the authorised agent account will also be accessible. To access the authorised agent account at any point, each person must use their own GOV.UK One Login.

The ACSP can then decide which users to add or remove, for example employees within the company secretarial team or corporate team of the firm. These people who work for the ACSP can be added to the account without needing to verify their own identity (although they will need their own Companies House account to access the authorised agents account). Once they have been added to the authorised agent account, such individuals will be able to access all the services for authorised agents when they log in to their own Companies House account i.e., they will be able to tell Companies House that they have verified someone's identity (and at a later stage, as discussed above, can file for clients using this authorised account).

As part of adding a user to the authorised agent account, the ACSP is required to allocate a role for each user on the account. There is currently a choice of three roles. As noted above, all users can sign into the account and access the list of the users for the ACSP and verify client's identities. The additional roles relate to running the authorised agent account (not the ACSP services used).

Firstly, users may be "account owners". As noted above, account owners can update the authorised agent's details (which must be done within fourteen days if any details have changed). They also have the power to add and remove all users of the account. An account owner can also close the authorised agent account. This service to "close the authorised agent" can also be accessed from the authorised agent's account.

The second role for users is an "administrator". Administrators can add and remove other administrators and any standard users.

The final role is a "standard user". This role has no ability to add or remove any other user (but as noted above, the term "standard" is a misnomer as such a user can still file at Companies House and verify identities). See the practical tip below in relation to this key point.

Account owners and administrators can remove users from the authorised agent account at any time and once they have been removed, they cannot access the account at all (or make any filings or verify any identities for the ACSP).

<u>Practical tip:</u>

It is vital to be aware that every user added to the account will be able to file on behalf of clients for Companies House AND will be able to tell Companies House that they have verified an individual's identity.

A risk policy should be put in place and training provided to **all users** of the authorised agent account before they are added to the authorised agent account as to what they are permitted (and not permitted) to do. This is vital for the protection of the firm and its officers.

If there are breaches in the use of the authorised agent account, see below as to who will be liable (but the key point is that it will not be the individual employees that are held to account by Companies House) but the officers and the firm that could suffer the consequences which are wide reaching.

If a firm has decided NOT to offer identity verification services, this must be controlled via policy, training and internal communications, as the authorised agent account will continue to permit all users to carry out this verification.

Who is liable for failure to comply with ACSP obligations?

There are wide reaching consequences for failure to comply with the legal obligations of the ACSP (which can go far beyond Companies House). It is necessary to establish who may be liable and what these liabilities may entail.

As noted above in relation to who can register as an ACSP, it is clear both sole traders and firms (such as companies and limited liability partnerships) can register as an ACSP.

If the ACSP is a sole trader, it will be the sole trader who bears the compliance responsibility. For all other business forms, all officers are responsible. For companies, this means it will be all the directors who bear the liability for failure to comply with ACSP obligations. For other forms of business media, it will be anyone whose roles correspond to directors (such as the members of a limited liability partnership).

This is a key issue that needs to be discussed with the firms' risk team as it will be the employees that make the filings etc. but the officers that bear the consequences for failure to comply (and some of the consequences can have far reaching implications for the practice) (see below).

Consequences of failure to comply with the legal requirements of an ACSP

Offence

The first consequence is that the ACSP will be guilty of an offence for failure to comply with their legal obligations set out above. Essentially this means that the sole trader, or all the company directors (and equivalent roles in other businesses) could be fined or be criminally prosecuted. It must be stressed that this is a personal liability for each of these officers, which can be deeply concerning.

Suspension

The next practical consequence is that the ACSP status as an authorised agent may be suspended. If Companies House is going to suspend an ACSP, they will email the ACSP to their correspondence email address provided on registration with next steps. If the ACSP is required to provide more information or documentation surrounding their filings, they will be given twenty-eight days to comply.

During this period, all users who were added to the ACSP authorised account will not be able to access any services, which practically means they cannot use the authorised account to file for clients or verify individuals during the period of the suspension. At this point, Companies House may contact anyone who the ACSP had verified identities for, and it may trigger a reverification request (see below).

The ACSP will also be added to the list of suspended agents (see Chapter 5 above) which shows the name of the firm, their status and the date they were suspended. As discussed in Chapter 5, it does not explain the reason for the suspension or provide any further information surrounding the suspension.

Both the publication of the firm's name (and also the reverification triggers) may also have significant reputational implications.

Cessation

After suspension, Companies House may also cease the ACSP status. The ACSP will be emailed at their correspondence email address with confirmation that the status as ACSP has been ceased and they are no longer an authorised agent for Companies House. The ACSP online account will be closed; and all users will no longer be able to access the account. As with suspension, the name of the ACSP will be published on the list of ceased agents, and again, it will only show the firm name, their status and the date of cessation. It does not explain the reason for the cessation or provide any further information surrounding the cessation. It will also potentially trigger reverification requests as with suspensions.

Cessation is a permanent measure and would mean the firm would be unable to use the authorised agent account to file or verify individual's identities for Companies House. There is currently no appeal process in place for cessation.

This could have a hugely detrimental impact on a firm's business if they rely on being able to incorporate companies or file forms or companies accounts for their clients.

Professional negligence/anti-money laundering supervisory consequences

Finally, in relation to consequences for the ACSP directly, if the criminal offence and suspension/cessation were not sufficient, Companies House is permitted to share data with the ACSP's anti-money laundering supervisor surrounding the breach/breaches. It may then be the case that the ACSP's anti-money laundering supervisor may take separate enforcement action against the ACSP (and it could also form the basis of a professional negligence action).

Trigger of reverification

If the consequences against the officers of the ACSP were not sufficient, it should also be noted that any suspension or cessation may also trigger consequences for the clients of the ACSP. It has been clear throughout this text that identity verification should usually be a one-off occurrence. However, there are circumstances where Companies House may give an individual who has previously had their identity verified a reverification notice.

A reverification notice may be served if Companies House has reasonable cause to believe that the information or evidence delivered by the ACSP to or relied on by Companies House for identity verification is misleading, false or deceptive in a material particular. The consequence of receiving a reverification notice is that the individual concerned is deemed to have ceased to be verified unless within the period of forty-two days beginning on the date on which notice is given, they provide the information requested or provide a reverification statement.

<u>Practical tips:</u>

Many firms are electing NOT to offer identity verification services due to the wide-reaching consequences (and concerns that they cannot achieve the required standards discussed in Chapter 7 below).

The risk of not being able to file documentation for clients is a key concern, particularly to accountancy firms for example who rely on being able to file clients' accounts.

The decision to verify or not verify should be taken with the key officers of the firm in conjunction with their risk and anti-money laundering team, insurers and data protection officers and must carefully consider any guidance provided by the relevant regulator.

Michelle Giddings (Head of AML, ICAEW Professional Standards Department aptly stated that "*directors are able to verify their own identity directly at Companies House and, for many individuals, it will be easy enough to do it themselves. Therefore, you always need to ask yourself why an individual has come to you to verify their identity, because there's a risk that those who don't want to reveal their identity might try to exploit ACSPs.*"

It must also be noted that identity verification is not the same as the anti-money laundering client due diligence (See Chapter 9 for more information on the key differences).

CHAPTER SEVEN

HOW TO COMPLY WITH VERIFICATION STANDARDS FOR CLIENTS

The standard to achieve

As discussed in Chapters above, the main concern for firms is the requirement to meet identity verification standards to ensure compliance with the legal responsibilities set out in Chapter 5.

Companies House has provided detailed guidance surrounding the checks which will be broken down into each step that must be followed below to ensure compliance with the verification standards required.

All the steps must be followed to ensure that the verification has been completed to the appropriate standard. As noted in below, this is not a risk-based exercise, so each step must be completed satisfactorily for each client that the ACSP elects to verify.

Identity Document Validation Technology ("IDVT") – Option 1

The ACSP will need to consider if they wish to use IDVT directly to verify individuals. (As discussed further below, if they are outsourcing the service to a third-party provider or platform, these providers tend to use IDVT themselves).

The Companies House standard does permit ASCPs to verify using IDVT.

IDVT is technology that can help the ACSP assess and establish the authenticity of identity documents and can automate the process of checking the documents required for identity verification for Companies House such as biometric passports and driving licences (see the discussion surrounding Option 1 below).

IDVT is not a replacement for an expert in detecting fraudulent documents; but they do allow for higher levels of accuracy than a manual check by employees which can both reduce risk and speed up the process.

Manual checks can be time consuming, potentially unreliable and use up a lot of administrative time as they may only be conducted by someone who is trained in detecting false documents by a specialist provider (see below).

It is useful to understand what IDVT can consist of (as there are many forms depending on the needs of the user). IDVT usually consists of firstly of a device that can scan the identity document (which include specialised passport and card reader, webcams scanners and smartphones). The device is then supported by software and a precedent library of identity documents (to act as a comparison against the identity documents that have been scanned).

The software analyses and checks the security features on the document and compares the image of the document against the precedent of the document. Algorithms then score the document to indicate if it is authentic or not. Some IDVT systems also conduct deeper checks, for example checking against other data sources, conduct imposter checks and can maintain secure records of the documents checked and can even inform individuals about the data being collected and enable them to consent and to provide an audit trail for both the individual and the relying party (which again, is useful should Companies House require further information).

For Option 1 for Companies House, IDVT must be used to validate the cryptographic features of the document provided (see below for the list of potential documents). Cryptographic features are essentially security features that correctly identity the person or organisation that issued the document. If the document does not contain cryptographic features (for example, non-chipped documents such as a UK driving licence), the IDVT must be able to validate the physical security features contained within the document to verify the document provided.

Practical tip:

Even if IDVT is utilised by the ACSP, merely scanning and checking the document does not achieve completion of the steps set out by Companies House (and detailed below).

Each step must be completed in full and the ACSP must ensure they can evidence each step has been completed. If the technology used conducts each step, the ACSP must be able to demonstrate this.

Third party platforms or providers

After conducting the risk analysis proposed in Chapter 5 above, many ACSPs have decided to use or are considering utilising commercial identity verification providers to carry out the verification on their behalf.

This means that the ACSP is still taking responsibility for the verification of the relevant individual but have opted to use a third-party platform to deliver the service. It is vital to recognise that, regardless of whether the ACSP uses a third-party platform, it will be the ACSP who may be suspended or ceased as an authorised agent if the identity verification checks do not achieve the standard required by Companies House.

Choosing an appropriate commercial identity provider to conduct the verification for an ACSP will involve the ACSP being satisfied that the provider in question meets the standard that they are held to, and the

ACSP (and not the third party) must decide if the required information provided by the individual being verified is true.

This means that the ACSP must confirm that the commercial provider completes all the steps set out in this Chapter (or has ascertained that the provider will only complete some of the steps and the ACSP must then ensure it completes the remaining steps). The ACSP must be able to explain and evidence why the ACSP has concluded that the steps the third-party provider took are appropriate and to provide any documentation that Companies House may request surrounding the verification.

Companies House will not recommend or endorse any third-party commercial provider or confirm whether any provider meats the appropriate standard.

> **Email response from the ACSP team at Companies House**
>
> *Thank you for your email.*
>
> *I am sorry but we cannot recommend any commercial identity providers or platforms.*
>
> *If you wish to use one of those services, you should do your own checks to ensure they meet the Companies House requirements.*
>
> *Please see the following link; How to meet Companies House identity verification standard – GOV.UK.*

Things to consider/questions to ask when selecting a commercial identity provider or platform (including a checklist)

If a third-party provider or platform is to be utilised, the ACSP in question must be satisfied it meets the requirements noted above.

It is not compulsory for a third-party platform or provider to answer all the questions or considerations suggested by this text. However, it would be prudent to consider each of these aspects below (and a checklist is provided to assist) when conducting a firm's risk analysis and selecting an appropriate provider for the firm.

No.	Question	Yes/No
1.	Has the platform or provider been certified by the UK Government's Digital Identity and Attributes Trust Framework (see below)?	
2.	Does the platform or provider expressly confirm they meet, achieve or align with the Companies House standards for verification?	
3.	Can the provider or platform check cryptographic features when the document contains a biometric chip?	
4.	Can the provider or platform check cryptographic features when the document does not contains a biometric chip?	
5.	Does the platform or provider offer additional support for any "hard to verify" individuals or for issues that need guidance?	

6.	Does the platform or provider request additional documentation (if original documentation does not meet the requirements)?	
7.	Does the platform or provider generate reports for Companies House (to enable the ACSP to comply with any requests for information)?	
8.	Does the platform or provider maintain a full and comprehensive audit trail (enabling the ACSP to comply with Step 5 set out below)?	
9.	How does the platform or provider use their technology to comply with all of the steps (for example Steps 3 and 4 below)?	
10.	What is the time frame for achieving successful verification?	
11.	What is the time frame where verification is not successful?	
12.	Will the provider assist in achieving verification or provide guidance on why it was not successful?	
13.	How does the onboarding fit with the firms existing processes?	
14.	Is the platform ready to use without any additional technology or set up (for example is additional software required or is it a cloud-based option that can be used immediately)?	

15.	Is there a bulk upload option available for multiple verifications?	
16.	What technology does the platform or provider offer (and are they able to confirm that the data is secure and the online platform has robust security) and that the data will not be shared with any other agencies?	
17.	What are the costs?	
18.	Are the costs transparent?	
19.	Is there a minimum monthly volume?	
20.	Is the ACSP tied in?	
21.	Is the process simple and user friendly/easy to use (for both the ACSP and the client)?	
22.	How does the client access the process (e.g. can it be accessed via a laptop or tablet and is it flexible)?	
23.	Will they offer a trial for the ACSP to attempt the process?	
24.	Are positive reviews of the service available? Are the reviewers in similar areas of business?	

UK Government's Digital Identity & Attributed Trust Framework – snapshot

This is the first framework under the Data (Use and Access) Act 2025, which has been designed to ensure digital identity and attribute services are certified against the framework which can then be independently certified to prove compliance.

They embed a set of rules and standards defining what a good digital identity looks like and is used for digital verification services certification from 1 July 2025. (It is not solely for identity verification for Companies House, for example it is applicable for right to work, right to rent and disclosure and barring service identity checks).

There is a statutory register available to check. Both the register and the framework are freely searchable and can be found in Chapter 10: Useful Link at Document Q.

A third-party platform or provider that is certified to this standard demonstrates that they are upholding good digital identity verification standards.

Steps to carry out for verification

Step 1: Ask for information about the person

The person must provide the information set out in the list below:

- Full name including any middle names together with any former names
- Date of birth

- Current home address

- Last twelve months address history

- Email address

Step 2: Obtain evidence to verify the person's identity

The ACSP must ask to see documents to verify the person's identity. Copies of these documents must be taken by the ACSP and must be kept for seven years from the date the ACSP completes the identity checks. These copies do not have to be provided to Companies House when the ACSP uses the service to tell Companies House that the ACSP has verified their identity (but information will be needed about the documents including document reference number (or equivalent), expiry date (if the document has one), and country of issue (if the document has one)).

The documents that the ACSP must obtain depends on which option the ACSP uses for checking the identity documents. To recap the detail above, Option 1 involves using IDVT that can validate the cryptographic features of the document and Option 2 involves a manual check.

As noted above, whichever option is used, all the steps set out must be completed (just checking the documents at this Step 2 is not sufficient to meet the Companies House standards.

Practical tip:

Urge the client not to send expired documents. Consider creating FAQs for clients for them to review before they send documents to you – include the documents required.

The ACSP cannot use as evidence documents that have expired (unless an exception is specified (see document list below). However, if a document does expire after the identity checks have been successfully completed, the client will not need to verify again.

The ACSP also cannot use as evidence foreign equivalents of documents where an issuing country or authority is specified.

Documentation to be provided under Option 1

Only ONE of the following photographic identity documents in the table below are required.

Document type	**Extra information**
A biometric or machine-readable passport, or an Irish passport card	These can be up to 6 months expired if the IDVT being utilised can still validate the cryptographic features. This therefore demonstrates an officer requiring verification may be based anywhere in the world.
A UK, Channel Islands, Isle of Man and EU photocard driving licence	Full or provisional licences are both acceptable.
An identity card with biometric information from the EU, Norway, Iceland or Liechtenstein	These can be up to 18 months expired
A UK biometric residence permit ("BRP")	

A UK biometric residence card ("BRC")	
A UK Frontier Worker permit	

Documentation to be provided under Option 2

This option must be utilised if the documents are being checked by a person (i.e. the ACSP is NOT using IDVT). This option applies whether the documents are being checked remotely or in person and the vital component is that the ACSP must be satisfied the process they are using is sufficient to validate the documents provided. This is obviously a key concern to ACSPs who undertake to check the documents themselves.

The client being verified must provide two documents, which comprise either two photographic identity documents from group A or one photographic identity document from group A and one document from group B.

Again, the client will need at least one photographic identity document from group A to utilise this method. In addition, if the client does not live in the UK, they must provide at least one government issued document.

Group A documents	**Group B documents** *The ACSP does not need to provide a document reference number, expiry date, or country of issue for documents from this group B.*
Passport or Irish passport card – these can be up to 18 months expired	Birth or adoption certificate

Identity card with biometric information from the EU, Norway, Iceland or Liechtenstein	Marriage or civil partnership certificate
UK biometric residence permit (BRP) – these can be up to 18 months expired	Non-photographic immigration document
UK biometric residence card (BRC)	Non-photographic visa
UK accredited PASS card	Non-photographic work permit
UK or EU driver digital tachograph card	Bank or building society statement
UK, Channel Islands, Isle of Man and EU photocard driving licence (full or provisional)	UK local authority or social housing rental agreement – this must be for the person's current address
UK HM Forces ID Card	Mortgage statement – this must be for the person's current address
UK HM Armed Forces Veteran Card	UK council tax statement – this must be for the person's current address
UK Frontier Worker permit	Utility bill – this must be for the person's current address
Photographic work permit (government issued)	

Photographic immigration document	
Photographic visa	
UK, Channel Islands and Isle of Man firearms licence	
Another type of photographic ID listed on PRADO (opens in a new tab) – such as a National Identity Card (Pakistan), crew member certificate (South Africa), or Permanent Resident Card (USA)	

Step 3: Check the evidence is real

Many third-party platforms use technology and automate this part of the process to validate the evidence. It is therefore this third step that causes consternation for ACSPs electing not to utilise third party providers or platforms. This check is designed to validate the documents provided to ensure they are real, genuine documents and have not been tampered with in any way.

If the documents are being checked by a person, this person must be trained in detecting false documents and be familiar with the guidance on examining identity documents to detect basic forgeries. (See Chapter 10: Useful Links at document F for the full guidance).

As above in relation to IDVT, Companies House will not recommend any training providers that meet their criteria. The training providers must follow the Home Office best practice guide. Any ACSP checking documents may also wish to review the guidance prepared by the National Document Fraud Unit on examining identity documents (See

Chapter 10: Useful Links at document F as noted above). This guidance is extremely useful and includes images of the documents, suggestions of equipment that is easy to obtain (for example magnifiers and ultraviolet light sources) which can enhance the ability to detect fraudulent documents (although again, the equipment is only effective if the user understands the documentation and the relevant security features). It also contains a list of basic checks that should be made that can highlight cause for concern.

The documents must be examined for any signs of tampering and the ACSP must query if there are any signs of damage to a document (particularly if the damage is in an area where personal details are shown). The ACSP must contact the issuing authority or another authoritative source to check if there are any concerns about a document (including contacting the applicable embassy if the concerns stem from a document issued by a country outside of the UK).

Step 4: Check it is a real identity, and it belongs to the person claiming it

This involves checking that the documents confirm the person's name and date of birth.

If the ACSP is utilising Option 1, they must also check that the cryptographic features on the document match the information provided by the person being verified.

It must also be checked that the person physically matches the photo that is on or goes with the document and that they are a real person. This mean if the ACSP is verifying the individual remotely, they will need to ensure that they can clearly see their face in real time to be able to compare with the photograph that is on the identity documents. Again, many third-party providers utilise technology such as facial recognition and can match the live image to the photograph included in the identity documents, which can go further in reducing the risk of identity fraud.

Step 4 is further intended to combat the risk of the ACSP accepting a synthetic identity introduced as an issue in Chapter 1 and explained further in the snapshot below.

Snapshot: What is synthetic identity theft?

Synthetic identity theft or synthetic identity fraud is sophisticated fraud, is one of the fastest growing types of identity theft and has been identified as one of the largest threats banks are currently facing, as it can evade traditional fraud detection systems.

A synthetic identity is a fake identity that on the face of it, appears legitimate but the person identified does not actually exist. The fraudsters create a brand new, fictitious identity blending real data such as national insurance numbers and names and addresses with fake information.

Once they have achieved creating a fictitious identity and credit profile, they then apply for credit cards and build an online history for the fraudulent accounts.

To reduce the risk of the ACSP accepting such a synthetic identity, they should exercise caution.

The ACSP should always ask to see additional documentation if the identity documents provided do not confirm their address history for the last twelve months and/or if they have changed their name. If they cannot provide documentation that confirms their address history or a name change, the ACSP must consider not continuing to verify this person's identity.

In addition, to ensure the identity belongs to a real person and not a synthetic identity, the ACSP should also ask to see evidence of activity you would expect, for example a bank or credit card statement to see recent transactions, utility or council tax bills sent to the home address provided by the individual, if their passport has been used recently or over time, insurance policy documents (that again, show the home address that was provided),

An ACSP is not under a duty to complete a verification check if they are not satisfied – it is the individual's responsibility to verify their identity. If they cannot verify due to missing documents (for example they have no acceptable identity documents), they will need to apply to get documents that will enable them to verify their identity. As illustrated in Chapter 3, there is the ability to apply for an extension to the verification deadlines (and one of the reasons for an additional discretionary extension is because the person has applied for identity documents).

If the ACSP cannot verify the individual's identity, they must still retain records of the evidence used and checks conducted for seven years.

<u>Step 5: Keep records of the identity checks.</u>

The ACSP must keep records for seven years from the date identity verification is completed, of all the evidence and information used to conduct the verification.

This includes copies of the documents checked, evidence of the identity checks completed and records of any failed verification attempts. This requirement applies even if the ACSP uses a third-party provider or platform to conduct the checks. (This is discussed above in relation to questions to ask a third-party provider or platform).

<u>Step 6: Decide if the ACSP can verify the person's identity</u>

The ACSP must decide if they are satisfied the person is who they claim to be and that the ACSP has been able to verify them to Companies House required standard.

If the ACSP decides they can verify their identity, the online service available via the ACSP's authorised account must be used to tell

Companies House the individual's details (set out in further detail in the verification statement box below), which documents were used to verify their identity (and how they were checked), give details of the documents used and confirm that the ACSP has completed the checks to verify their identity to the required standard. This is known as the ACSP verification statement.

Verification statement from ACSP must:

- State the name of the individual to which it relates (as it is shown on at least one of the documents provided);

- Whether the documents were checked via Option 1 (IDVT) or by a person;

- State the date on which the ACSP became satisfied that the required personal information is true, the person is who they claim to be and that the ACSP has completed the identity checks that meet the Companies House identity verification standard; and

- Include a statement confirming that the ACSP has delivered or is delivering at the same time as the statement, the information referred to in regulation 11 (provision of information upon delivery of verification statement and reverification statement).

The information referred to in regulation 11 is the individual's date of birth, the required contact information which is the persons home address and an email address (which Companies House will use to send their personal code to), a description of the information and evidence which formed the basis on which the ACSP became satisfied that the required personal information is true (i.e. which documents the ACSP used as evidence including the document reference number, expiry date and country of issue), and the ACSP's unique identifier.

Practical tips:

Printing

It is important to print or save a copy of this verification statement submitted. Companies House will show the identity verification details submitted on the submission confirmation page – ensure this is printed or saved for the ACSP records.

Privacy Policy

All firms undertaking ACSP services should also review their privacy policy under UK GDPR.

If a firm is intending on verifying clients' identities, it must ensure that the firm's privacy policy clearly discloses to third parties that the firm may share data as part of the process of identity verification. If the firm's privacy policy is more generic, it should be checked carefully to ensure that the policy covers identity verification including the requirement that some data must be kept under the legislation for set periods.

In addition, if Option 1 (IDVT – see Chapter 7) is being utilised by a firm, it is also likely that the firm will need to store biometric data. This is a special category of data under UK GDPR, and therefore the firm is likely to be required to put in place more robust data security measures which are beyond the scope of this text.

It is strongly recommended for the team dealing with identity verification to liaise closely with the firm's data protection officer to ensure they are aware of the data being collected and retained and that the policies and security measures in place are appropriate for the firm's needs.

What happens if an ACSP makes an error within the verification statement

On 7 January 2026, an amendment was made to Volume 1 of The Registrar's (Requirements Applicable to Electronic Form Documents) Rules 2022. This came into force on 9 January 2026 and illustrates it is possible to correct identity verification details.

The amendment sets out in Schedule 11 that the relevant form may only be delivered and authenticated by the ACSP or an employee of the ACSP who delivered the original information that is intended to be replaced. The link to the online form can be found in Chapter 10: Useful Links at document S (and does illustrate that an ACSP can replace incorrect information included in an ACSP verification statement), which may come as a relief to ACSPs.

To proceed with a correction, the ACSP will need to complete their ACSP number, the verification reference (which will be contained on the confirmation email sent out by Companies House when the ACSP verified them), which details need to be corrected and what they should be and critically, the reason the details were entered incorrectly.

If it is a date of birth that requires correction, as discussed in previous chapters, evidence will be required to be uploaded showing the correct date (for example an image of the individuals passport or other identity document). Companies House also reserves the right to contact the ACSP if they need to ask for more information or further evidence.

At the time of publishing, this form and ability to make amendments is extremely new, therefore limited information is available surrounding any further requests Companies House may make.

CHAPTER EIGHT

KEY DIFFERENCES BETWEEN ANTI MONEY LAUNDERING CHECKS AND IDENTITY VERIFICATION

One common complaint from clients has been that there is a duplication of requirements upon them. They have already provided their identity documents to their professional advisors at the outset of their relationship for compliance with anti-money laundering regulations (which may include verification); they do not appreciate why their professional advisors cannot use these existing documents to confirm their identity with Companies House.

The way to respond to requests such as these is to explain that the identity verification process is not the same as checks required for anti-money laundering purposes and firms existing anti money laundering processes will not meet the requirements placed upon ACSPs. The impact assessment discussed in Chapter 4 analysed this issue and reiterated that anti money laundering checks verify a customer rather than verifying a director or PSC and to achieve verification, ACSPs will need to ensure they are achieving the same standards as those checks undertaken by Companies House when individuals verify directly.

ICAS (the global professional membership organisation and business network for Chartered Accountants) published an article on 18 April 2025 that reiterates this key point, agreeing that it is not the case that the identity verification process used by firms for anti-money laundering purposes is sufficient for ACSP purposes. Identity verification for Companies House is a fixed process which is the same for all individuals. Anti-money laundering customer due diligence is risk based and varies from client to client. ICAS full guidance is set out in Chapter 10: Useful Links, document L.

More specific differences between the two are set out below.

Firstly, identity verification requires either training in the use of the technology in Option 1 or Option 2 requires that the documents produced are examined by a person trained in document examination in accordance with the Home Office guidance (discussed in Chapter 7 above). The requirements under the money laundering regulations do not contain this.

We have noted in this text that identity verification impacts all companies (and all officers). Some accountancy bodies may approach the money laundering identity verification on a risk-based approach, which practically may mean that only some of the directors and PSCs may be verified for a client. In addition, the information required to be gathered for identity verification is more extensive whilst the document list for Option 2 is more restrictive than the documents that may be used for anti-money laundering checks.

Lastly, ACSPs must also retain the identity verification documents for a lengthier period than required for the anti-money laundering checks as discussed in Chapter 7 above, even if the ACSP failed to verify the client's identity.

CHAPTER NINE

CONCLUSIONS AND FUTURE DEVELOPMENTS

The vision set out in the Companies Huse strategy 2025 to 2030 is that "*by 2030 Companies House will be the trusted guardian of corporate transparency, acting as a catalyst for economic growth, while protecting business and people from harm*".

The ECCTA is huge driver to achieving this vision and is one of the largest changes to company law since the implementation of Companies Act 2006. The introduction of identity verification has unquestionably raised the bar for compliance in terms of corporate transparency by improving the public registers, integrating GOV.UK One Login and forcing mandatory identity verification (which cannot be completed without ensuring correct details are registered at Companies House), together with increasing accountability for those responsible for making filings at Companies House.

Many corporate secretarial teams have noted that it has increased the administrative burden for example ensuring that they have collated and stored their clients' personal codes accurately and in a timely manner, allowing them to file required forms on time.

It has also placed the onus on ensuring details are correct when filings are made on the relevant individual (for example, typographical errors when incorporating a company now have wide reaching consequences as a simple error on a date of birth will mean that the identity verification details will not link to the person and the filing will not be processed).

It does mean that the data on the public register will start to become more robust and accurate as there are a significant number of individuals who are required to make corrections prior to completing identity verification successfully.

As of January 2025, only one million individuals out of the seven million who are caught by the legislation had verified their identity, meaning just over 85% of individuals had not yet completed the task.

Quarterly management data on the number and percentage of director and PSC appointments that complied with identity verification for the period between October and December 2025 showed a worryingly low percentage at that point. The percentage of appointments verified was as low as 6.27% (and it is worth bearing in mind that many individuals have more than one appointment, so the number of verified appointments will not equal the number of verified individuals).

One year later, by 22 January 2026, this figure had increased to more than two and a half million people who have been issued personal codes after successfully verifying their identity.

Over time, this percentage should continue to increase (and the Companies House management data will be released on a quarterly basis to publish these percentages) and Companies House have also already indicated their willingness to act for incorrect filings. It illustrates that the requirement to create a verified Companies House digital identity and link it to filings should go much further in preventing the future misuse of companies in the UK. Companies House have also stated on 22 January 2026 that their key focus for 2026 is to complete identity verification for everyone caught by the legislation and they are on track to achieve this.[9]

There are also numerous ways both the data and experience can be improved and various statutory gaps filled. Some have already been

9 Becoming the trusted guardian of corporate transparency – 22 January 2026, Andy King

addressed, such as originally there was to be no publicly available list of registered ACSPs, and this has now been changed.

This text has highlighted several gaps it is keen to see improved (for example being unable to see any reasons behind suspension or cessation of an ACSP) and the ongoing issues with filing for groups. The longer the requirement to verify is in force, the more it is hoped that these gaps will be addressed by secondary legislation.

Despite the gaps (and the administrative burden for many combined with the increased filing costs), the legislation has undoubtably already served to improve the quality and reliability of the data available at Companies House and Andy King's goal of by "*2030, we want to be known as the trusted guardian of corporate transparency. That means when someone looks up a UK company anywhere in the world, they can be confident the information they're seeing is accurate, up-to-date, and reliable*" seems much more achievable.[10]

[10] Companies House strategy: Building trust in our data, cracking down on economic crime and supporting growth, 23 October 2025

CHAPTER TEN

USEFUL LINKS

Letter ref:	Document:	Weblink:
A.	Companies House email updates subscription link	https://public.govdelivery.com/accounts/UKCH/subscriber/new
B.	Company authentication codes for online filing	https://www.gov.uk/guidance/company-authentication-codes-for-online-filing
C.	Changes to UK Company Law Campaign website	https://changestoukcompanylaw.campaign.gov.uk/
D.	Collection of guidance for ACSPs	https://www.gov.uk/government/collections/services-for-authorised-corporate-service-providers
E.	Full list of UK anti-money laundering supervisory bodies	https://www.gov.uk/anti-money-laundering-registration
F.	Guidance on examining identity documents to detect basic forgeries	https://www.gov.uk/government/publications/recognising-fraudulent-identity-documents

G.	Guidance on verifying your identity for Companies House	https://www.gov.uk/guidance/verifying-your-identity-for-companies-house
H.	Guidance on when you need to verify your identity	https://www.gov.uk/guidance/when-you-need-to-verify-your-identity-for-companies-house
I.	How to apply to register as an ACSP	https://find-and-update.company-information.service.gov.uk/register-as-companies-house-authorised-agent
J.	How to find your personal code (video)	https://youtu.be/x_X1VutKyxo
K.	How to obtain an Experian credit report	https://www.experian.co.uk/experian-account/01_free_score.html
L.	ICAS guidance on the difference between anti money laundering and identity verification	https://www.icas.com/news-insights-events/news/practice/are-identity-requirements-the-same-for-anti-money-laundering-and-companies-house-purposes
M.	List of ACSPs	https://www.gov.uk/government/publications/list-of-authorised-corporate-service-providers-acsps

N.	Policy paper – Economic Crime and Corporate Transparency Act: outline transition plan for Companies House	https://www.gov.uk/government/publications/economic-crime-and-corporate-transparency-act-outline-transition-plan-for-companies-house/economic-crime-and-corporate-transparency-act-outline-transition-plan-for-companies-house
O.	Provide identity verification details for a PSC service	https://www.gov.uk/guidance/provide-psc-verification
P.	Request an extension for a PSC	https://submit.forms.service.gov.uk/form/262187/request-to-extend-the-identity-verification-deadline-for-a-psc/4GWbjwfm
Q.	UK Digital Identity Services Register Framework	https://www.digital-identity-services-register.service.gov.uk/
R.	WebFiling access	https://ewf.companieshouse.gov.uk/runpage?page=oauthSignIn
S.	Correction to identity verification details	https://submit.forms.service.gov.uk/form/8629/correct-someone-s-identity-verification-details/GiD648pc

MORE BOOKS BY LAW BRIEF PUBLISHING

A selection of our other titles available now:-

'A Practical Guide to Probation Breaches and Other Applications' by Mark Thomas
'A Practical Guide to Remarriage and Divorce' by Cordelia Williams & Claire Howard
'A Practical Guide to Privacy, Transparency, Reporting Restrictions and Closed Proceedings in the Court of Protection' by Laura Mannering
'Beaumont on Barristers – A Guide to Defending Disciplinary Proceedings (Second Edition)' by Marc Beaumont
'A Practical Guide to Payments for Environmental Services' by Ben Sharples
'A Practical Guide to the Law of Pregnancy and Maternity at Work' by Rebecca Thomas
'A Practical Guide to Redundancy – Second Edition' by Philip Hyland & Collette Moore
'A Practical Guide to International Issues for Scottish Family Lawyers' by Susie Mountain, Donna McKay, Ken MacDonald
'A Practical Guide to the Law on Deprivation of Liberty' by Ben Troke
'A Practical Guide to Rights over Airspace and Subsoil – Second Edition' by Daniel Gatty
'A Practical Guide to the Law in Relation to Inquests' by Ramya Nagesh
'A Practical Guide to the Construction and Rectification of Wills and Trust Instruments (Second Edition)' by Edward Hewitt
'A Practical Guide to Data Protection in Social Housing' by Clare Paterson
'A Practical Guide to Spousal Maintenance – Second Edition' by Liz Cowell
'A Practical Guide to International Parental Child Abduction Law (England and Wales)' by Dr Onyója Momoh
'A Practical Guide to Deprivation of British Citizenship' by Sean Ell
'A Practical Guide to Commercial Property Service Charges' by Rachel Garton
'A Practical Guide to Clinical Negligence – Third Edition' by Geoffrey Simpson-Scott (Geoff)
'A Practical Guide to the Rights of Grandparents in Children Proceedings – Second Edition' by Stuart Barlow

‘The Electronic Communications Code: A Practical Guide – Second Edition’ by Kerry Bretherton KC, James Castle, Mark Loveday
‘A Practical Guide to the Independent School Standards – September 2023 Edition’ by Sarah McKimm
'A Practical Guide to Estate Administration and Crypto Assets' by Richard Marshall
‘A Practical Guide to Parental Alienation in Private and Public Law Children Cases’ by Sam King QC & Frankie Shama
‘Contested Heritage – Removing Art from Land and Historic Buildings’ by Richard Harwood QC, Catherine Dobson, David Sawtell
‘The Limits of Separate Legal Personality: When Those Running a Company Can Be Held Personally Liable for Losses Caused to Third Parties Outside of the Company’ by Dr Mike Wilkinson
‘A Practical Guide to Transgender Law’ by Robin Moira White & Nicola Newbegin
‘A Practical Guide to ‘Stranded Spouses’ in Family Law’ by Mani Singh Basi
‘A Practical Guide to Residential Freehold Conveyancing’ by Lorraine Richardson
‘A Practical Guide to Pensions on Divorce for Lawyers’ by Bryan Scant
‘A Practical Guide to Challenging Sham Marriage Allegations in Immigration Law’ by Priya Solanki
‘A Practical Guide to Digital Communications Evidence in Criminal Law’ by Sam Willis
‘A Practical Guide to Legal Rights in Scotland’ by Sarah-Jane Macdonald
‘A Practical Guide to New Build Conveyancing’ by Paul Sams & Rebecca East
‘A Practical Guide to Inherited Wealth on Divorce’ by Hayley Trim
‘A Practical Guide to Practice Direction 12J and Domestic Abuse in Private Law Children Proceedings’ by Rebecca Cross & Malvika Jaganmohan
‘A Practical Guide to Confiscation and Restraint’ by Narita Bahra QC, John Carl Townsend, David Winch
‘A Practical Guide to the Law of Forests in Scotland’ by Philip Buchan
‘A Practical Guide to Health and Medical Cases in Immigration Law’ by Rebecca Chapman & Miranda Butler
‘A Practical Guide to Bad Character Evidence for Criminal Practitioners by Aparna Rao
‘A Practical Guide to Extradition Law post-Brexit’ by Myles Grandison et al
‘A Practical Guide to Hoarding and Mental Health for Housing Lawyers’ by Rachel Coyle

'Stephens on Contractual Indemnities' by Richard Stephens

'A Practical Guide to the EU Succession Regulation' by Richard Frimston

'A Practical Guide to Solicitor and Client Costs – Second Edition' by Robin Dunne

'Constructive Dismissal – Practice Pointers and Principles' by Benjimin Burgher

'A Practical Guide to Religion and Belief Discrimination Claims in the Workplace' by Kashif Ali

'A Practical Guide to the Law of Medical Treatment Decisions' by Ben Troke

'Fundamental Dishonesty and QOCS in Personal Injury Proceedings: Law and Practice' by Jake Rowley

'A Practical Guide to the Law in Relation to School Exclusions' by Charlotte Hadfield & Alice de Coverley

'A Practical Guide to Divorce for the Silver Separators' by Karin Walker

'The Right to be Forgotten – The Law and Practical Issues' by Melissa Stock

'A Practical Guide to Planning Law and Rights of Way in National Parks, the Broads and AONBs' by James Maurici QC, James Neill et al

'A Practical Guide to Election Law' by Tom Tabori

'A Practical Guide to the Law in Relation to Surrogacy' by Andrew Powell

'A Practical Guide to Claims Arising from Fatal Accidents – Second Edition' by James Patience

'A Practical Guide to Asbestos Claims' by Jonathan Owen & Gareth McAloon

'A Practical Guide to Stamp Duty Land Tax in England and Northern Ireland' by Suzanne O'Hara

'A Practical Guide to the Law of Farming Partnerships' by Philip Whitcomb

'A Practical Guide to the Law of Unlawful Eviction and Harassment – Second Edition' by Stephanie Lovegrove

'A Practical Guide to Costs in Personal Injury Claims – Second Edition' by Matthew Hoe

'A Practical Guide to the General Data Protection Regulation (GDPR) – Second Edition' by Keith Markham

'A Practical Guide to Working with Litigants in Person and McKenzie Friends in Family Cases' by Stuart Barlow

'Protecting Unregistered Brands: A Practical Guide to the Law of Passing Off' by Lorna Brazell

'A Practical Guide to Secondary Liability and Joint Enterprise Post-Jogee' by Joanne Cecil & James Mehigan

'A Practical Guide to the Pre-Action RTA Claims Protocol for Personal Injury Lawyers' by Antonia Ford
'A Practical Guide to Neighbour Disputes and the Law' by Alexander Walsh
'A Practical Guide to Coercive Control for Legal Practitioners and Victims' by Rachel Horman
'A Practical Guide to the Law of Driverless Cars – Second Edition'
by Alex Glassbrook, Emma Northey & Scarlett Milligan
'A Practical Guide to TOLATA Claims' by Greg Williams
'A Practical Guide to Elderly Law – Second Edition' by Justin Patten
'A Practical Guide to Responding to Housing Disrepair and Unfitness Claims' by Iain Wightwick
'A Practical Guide to the Law of Bullying and Harassment in the Workplace' by Philip Hyland
'How to Be a Freelance Solicitor: A Practical Guide to the SRA-Regulated Freelance Solicitor Model' by Paul Bennett
'A Practical Guide to Prison Injury Claims' by Malcolm Johnson
'A Practical Guide to Advising Clients at the Police Station' by Colin Stephen McKeown-Beaumont
'A Practical Guide to Antisocial Behaviour Injunctions – Second Edition' by Iain Wightwick
'Practical Mediation: A Guide for Mediators, Advocates, Advisers, Lawyers, and Students in Civil, Commercial, Business, Property, Workplace, and Employment Cases' by Jonathan Dingle with John Sephton
'The Mini-Pupillage Workbook' by David Boyle
'A Practical Guide to Crofting Law' by Brian Inkster
'A Practical Guide to the Law of Domain Names and Cybersquatting' by Andrew Clemson
'A Practical Guide to the Law of Gender Pay Gap Reporting' by Harini Iyengar
'NHS Whistleblowing and the Law' by Joseph England
'Employment Law and the Gig Economy' by Nigel Mackay & Annie Powell
'A Practical Guide to Noise Induced Hearing Loss (NIHL) Claims' by Andrew Mckie, Ian Skeate, Gareth McAloon
'An Introduction to Beauty Negligence Claims – A Practical Guide for the Personal Injury Practitioner' by Greg Almond
'Intercompany Agreements for Transfer Pricing Compliance' by Paul Sutton
'Zen and the Art of Mediation' by Martin Plowman
'A Practical Guide to Adoption for Family Lawyers' by Graham Pegg

'A Practical Guide to Industrial Disease Claims' by Andrew Mckie & Ian Skeate

'A Practical Guide to Conducting a Sheriff Court Proof' by Andrew Stevenson

'A Practical Guide to Vicarious Liability' by Mariel Irvine

'A Practical Guide to Applications for Landlord's Consent and Variation of Leases' by Mark Shelton

'A Practical Guide to Relief from Sanctions Post-Mitchell and Denton' by Peter Causton

'A Practical Guide to Equity Release for Advisors' by Paul Sams

'A Practical Guide to Financial Services Claims' by Chris Hegarty

'A Practical Guide to Financial Ombudsman Service Claims' by Adam Temple & Robert Scrivenor

'A Practical Guide to Running Housing Disrepair and Cavity Wall Claims – Second Edition' by Andrew Mckie & Ian Skeate

'A Practical Guide to Holiday Sickness Claims – Second Edition' by Andrew Mckie & Ian Skeate

'Arguments and Tactics for Personal Injury and Clinical Negligence Claims' by Dorian Williams

'A Practical Guide to Drone Law' by Rufus Ballaster, Andrew Firman, Eleanor Clot

'On Experts: CPR35 for Lawyers and Experts' by David Boyle

'An Introduction to Personal Injury Law' by David Boyle

These books and more are available to order online direct from the publisher at www.lawbriefpublishing.com, where you can also read free sample chapters. For any queries, call us on 0844 587 2383 or email us at mail@lawbriefpublishing.com.

Our books are all generally in stock at www.amazon.co.uk with free next day delivery for Prime members, and at good legal bookshops such as Wildy & Sons.

We are regularly launching new books in our series of practical day-to-day practitioners' guides. Visit our website and join our free newsletter to be kept informed and to receive special offers, free chapters, etc.

You can also follow us on Twitter at www.twitter.com/lawbriefpub.

www.ingramcontent.com/pod-product-compliance
Lightning Source LLC
LaVergne TN
LVHW022113200926
848481LV00003B/1162
9781918241235